CAROL RUMENS was born and brought up in London. She is a freelance writer and held several writing fellowships in England before being appointed writer-in-residence at Queen's University Belfast in 1991, and subsequently at University College Cork in 1996. She has partially settled in Northern Ireland and currently divides her time between Belfast and London. A leading poet, she has published eleven volumes of poetry, edited various anthologies, and translated poems from Russian. Her most recent books include *Thinking of Skins: New Selected Poems* (1993), *Best China Sky* (1995) and *The Miracle Diet* (1997). She is currently the editor of an occasional literary magazine, *Brangle*, and is completing an M.Phil. at Queen's University.

holding pattern
carol rumens

THE
BLACKSTAFF
PRESS

BELFAST

• A BLACKSTAFF PRESS PAPERBACK ORIGINAL •

Blackstaff Paperback Originals present new writing, previously unpublished in Britain and Ireland, at an affordable price.

ACKNOWLEDGEMENTS

Acknowledgements are due to the editors of the following publications, in which some of the poems in Part II first appeared: *Acumen, As Girls Could Boast* (Oscars Press, London 1994), *HU, Fortnight, The Forward Book of Poetry 1998* (Forward Publishing, London 1997), the *New Yorker, Poetry Ireland Review, Poetry London Newsletter, Poetry Review, Times Literary Supplement, Verse*.
The poem 'A Singer Too Soon' was published in a pamphlet, *Coming Home (Powrót do Domu)*, edited and with English translations by Jerzy Jarniewicz (British Council, Poland 1998). 'The Burial' appeared as a poem-poster in an exhibition on London buses, sponsored by Big Wide Words and Friends of the Earth in 1997.
I would particularly like to thank Bloodaxe Books for their kind permission to reprint material from *Thinking of Skins* (1993) and *Best China Sky* (1995).

First published in 1998 by
The Blackstaff Press Limited
3 Galway Park, Dundonald, Belfast BT16 2AN, Northern Ireland
with the assistance of
The Arts Council of Northern Ireland

© Carol Rumens, 1998
All rights reserved

Carol Rumens has asserted her right under the
Copyright, Designs and Patents Act 1988 to be identified as
the author of this work.

Typeset by Techniset Typesetters, Newton-le-Willows, Merseyside

Printed in Ireland by ColourBooks Limited

A CIP catalogue record for this book
is available from the British Library

ISBN 0-85640-638-4

*In loving memory of my father
Wilfred Arthur Lumley
1911–1979*

CONTENTS

I *Poems from*
 THINKING OF SKINS *and* BEST CHINA SKY

The Lost Language of Birth	3
The Fuchsia Knight	4
Sunday Evening, Belfast 9	5
Stealing the Genre	7
Chippa Rippa	10
Variant Readings	11
Visions of a Protestant	12
Dreams of Revolution	13
Intruders	14
Schoolgirl's Story	15
The Lisburn Road List	16
Snowfire	18
Head Cold	19
Et Incarnatus Est	20
Genius Loci	22
Clouding the Borders	24
Curriculum Poetica	25
Antrim Road Dream-House	27
A Small Incendiary Device on Eglantine Avenue	28
Two Windowscapes	29
Summer Time Begins	31
The First Storytellers	32
Tír Fá Tonn	33

Iris and the Hailstone	34
Best China Sky	35
Prayer for Northern Ireland	36

II HOLDING PATTERN

Stanzas for a New Start	39
Kilkenny Castle	40
Raglan Weir	41
My Dark Windows	43
A Hiccup in the History of Belfast	45
St Peter's Welcomes the Peace Walkers	47
Old Friend, New Address	49
A Singer Too Soon	50
Boating in a Border County	51
Winter Travel	53
Absent Weatherwomen	54
The Island	55
From a Lexicon of Unlikely Couples	56
To Poetry	57
Housewarming	58
To Break House Rules	59
Promethean	60
Strange Wounds	61
The Burial	62
Where the Rainbow Ends	63
A Label	64
Spark City	66
No Man's Land	69
Characters	70
White-watching in Cork City	71
Conversation with a Sea Gull	72
Sister Love	74

A Day in the Life of Farmer Dream	75
Autumn Haiku	76
Thirst for Green	78
An Answer	80
Words	81
A Feast of Epiphany	82
Sybil Yawns	83
Two Belfast Beasts	84
The Photophobe	86
Ghost Story	87
Street Snapshots in a New Peacetime	88
Long Shot	89
Tea on the Fifth of July	90
The Song of Jack Flag	91
Words for Politicians	92
To His Coy Mistress, From Beyond the Grave	94
Fresh Garbage	96
Stitches in Time	97
The Lightest Dancer	99
Song of the Gsohs	100
Insight in Lavery's	101
Dilemma	102
Riddle	103
Céilí in Belfast 9	104
Sans Souci Flats	105
Chrisnin Gifts	106
Round Trip	108
Ineducable	109
Holding Pattern	110

ISLANDS

I had just started in the first year of grammar school. We sat at old-fashioned paired desks. To punish me for chattering and inattention, the form teacher had a single desk brought into the classroom and placed directly opposite her own desk. Here I would be stranded for the rest of the year. I daren't turn round and talk to my friends and they daren't talk to me. Most of our lessons were held in that room, and so I gradually lost the habit of conversation. My marks got even worse. I sat in a world of daydreams, cultivating a solitary aloof bitterness, with a sweetener or two of self-pity. The tyrant at her large desk ceased to notice me at my small one. Since then I have always preferred small islands to large.

I

Poems from
THINKING OF SKINS
and
BEST CHINA SKY

THE LOST LANGUAGE OF BIRTH

To be here, to be nowhere, nervous as the wind
Or the landing-lights at ten thousand feet,
Systole, diastole, hanging by a thread

Over the reticent, brick-humble streets
(Which turn their backs on me like men not guilty,
Not going anywhere, their eyes hilly):

To be dropped in my own pocket, my own excuses.
To muscle in on the lough like a sea breeze,
Mountainous hands arranging the hip bones wide

For that great loneliness, birth. To walk across carpets
I must have stolen, out of my rooms that drain
The natural colour from my children's faces.

To learn which side of the sun death lives, yet love
The youngest tones of white, from blush to faintness:
To be any datable girl, pushing fists, elbows

And all she has through the breathy lycra climate,
Emerging sleeked and open-mouthed, the glass
Split by forbidden words like 'swan', like 'girl'.

THE FUCHSIA KNIGHT

You gathered his yarn onto unfamiliar looms,
And the vowels you dropped, the soft-signs you appended,
Brindled the cloth and changed it, like the tears
Forged in the hedgerows, bending the thick stems
With weights not even a god deserves to weep.

You bore him flowers which seemed so abundantly
Indigenous, he forgot his planter's rank.
His head grew misty with heather: luminous roses
And the never-heard song of his native nightingale
Brimmed between him and his sword. He learned to drink

Your consonants with childish intensity
As you chased them towards him with a dry-lipped stammer
Less part of the need for love than the search for perfection.
He learned that to open the veins of speech is sometimes
To unzip the fuchsia linings of live skin.

SUNDAY EVENING, BELFAST 9

The family cars pour with a limousine swish
Down the sequestered avenue, their style
Not quite at ease, still conscious of arrival
And settlement in this almost solid parish.
Their careful drivers dipped as carefully to
The service, dropped the occasional autumn cough,
Then rose, shook hands, went fed and gilded through
A trace of mist, impatient to be off.
Under familiar trees at last, they bring
Magnified, watery shadows of good news
To driveways flooded with the shine of home,
And let the ritual die. A dog barks welcome.
The gravel settles down after applauding
Their buoyant tyres, the highlights of their shoes.

Were their mild hopes alerted, for a mute
Second, as creed went naked on the street?
Walking the other side, I could have slipped
From any congregation save their own:
No stranger's guaranteed in a darkening town.
But I proved harmless, too. I'd read the pavement
And found the place where all the petals, blown
From yesterday's weddings, might have been translucent
Evidence of imaginary bushes,

Their everlasting roses specially bred
To shower a bride in delicate, soundless wishes.
I picked them out, like moonlight from stained glass,
Like glass from skin, waiting to cross the road,
Thinking: the gods will pass, *the gods will pass*.

STEALING THE GENRE

It was the shortest night of the year. I'd been drinking
But I was quite lucid and calm. So, having seen her
The other side of the bar, shedding her light
On no one who specially deserved it, I got to my feet
And simply went over and asked her, in a low voice,
If she'd come to my bed. She raised her eyebrows strangely
But didn't say no. I went out. I felt her follow.

My mind was a storm as we silently crossed the courtyard
In the moist white chill of the dawn. Dear God, I loved her.
I'd loved her in books, I'd adored her at the first sighting.
But no, I'm a woman, English, not young. How could I?
She'd vanished for years. And now she was walking beside me.
Oh what am I going to do, what are *we* going to do?
Perhaps she'll know. She's probably an old hand –
But this sudden thought was the most disturbing of all.

As soon as we reached my room, though, it was plain
She hadn't a clue. We stood like window displays
In our dawn-damp suits with the short, hip-hugging skirts
(Our styles are strangely alike, I suppose it's because
Even she has to fight her corner in a man's world)
And discussed the rain, which was coming down, and the view,
Which was nothing much, a fuchsia hedge and some trees,

7

And we watched each other, as women do watch each other,
And tried not to yawn. Why don't you lie down for a bit?
I whispered, inspired. She gratefully kicked off her shoes.

She was onto the bed in no time, and lay as if dumped
On the furthest edge, her face – dear God – to the wall.
I watched for a while, and, thinking she might be in tears,
Caressed the foam-padded viscose that passed for her shoulder,
And begged her not to feel guilty. Then I discovered
That all she was doing was breathing, dead to the world.

It wasn't an insult, exactly, but it was a let-down –
And yet I admired her. Sleep. If only I could.
I rested my hand at an uncontroversial location
South of her breasts, maybe north, I don't remember,
And ached with desire and regret and rationalisation.
I'd asked her to bed. And she'd come to bed. End of story.
Only it wasn't the story I'd wanted to tell.
Roll on, tomorrow, I urged, but tomorrow retorted:
I'm here already, and nothing ever gets better.

But then, unexpectedly, I began to feel pleased.
To think she was here, at my side, so condensed, so weighty!
In my humble position (a woman, English, not young,
Et cetera) what more could I ask of an Irish dawn
Than this vision, alive, though dead to the world, on my duvet?
What have I done to deserve her? Oh, never mind,
Don't think about words like 'deserve'. So we lay in grace.
The light. Her hair. My hand. Her breath. And the fuchsias.
I thought of the poem I'd write, and fell asleep, smiling.

I woke in a daze of sublime self-congratulation
And saw she was gone. My meadow, my cloud, my aisling!
I could hardly believe my own memory. I wanted to scream
All over the courtyard, come back, come to bed, but how could I?
She might be anywhere, people were thick in the day
Already, and things were normal. Why are things normal?

I keened her name to the walls, I swam bitterest rivers,
I buried my face in the cloth where her blushes had slipped
And left a miraculous print that would baffle the laundry:
Oh let me die now. And the dark was all flame as I drank
The heart-breaking odour of Muguets des Bois and red wine –
Hers, though I have to admit, it could have been mine.

CHIPPA RIPPA
for Elena Semenliyska

Re-wakened memory-sound: the rustly chip and chock
As the poker rummages: the obedient mutter
And gush of the stirred coal, relinquishing
Its ardent childhood wish – to be immortal.

VARIANT READINGS

I expected bleachworks and burnt-out cars, not fuchsias:
Not cedar and sky-trickling larch, their remote massed shade,
Nor to hear my footsteps, lonely in streets of wet hedges
That tell me: here peace, and love, and money, are made.

Home was like this long ago, but can't be again.
I'll have chosen guilt and illusion, if I choose this
Most English of Irelands, our difference seemingly less
Than that between neighbourly hedges, depths of green.

VISIONS OF A PROTESTANT

I saw a city paved with stretched-out people.
They were clothed but their feet, for safety's sake, were bare.
Toes nestled lightly in all colours of hair,
Fingers in fingers. It was a jigsaw puzzle
Solved in heart pains, headaches, watering eyes:
Death shrank to a speck on a cliff of sighs.

I heard a city drowned in crystal thunder.
After a moment's silence, passionate saws
Were arguing chipboard into doors and windows.
A chalk stick stumbled, broke itself in two.
Prices slashed, it screamed, business as usual:
The speck was a huge, cruel face. The crowd walked tall.

DREAMS OF REVOLUTION

She's walking somewhere unresolved, sea-ravished,
Taking the flesh-tints of the facing sky
Among the stones, distributing them in water
Because there are no poor, now, in the village.

This is her lover's name-delighted classroom.
His finger prints a chalk-rose on her wrist
And leads her eyes to where a migrant shimmer
Of cursive vanishes on the rinsed slate.

He doesn't mind her townee misconceptions.
He scarcely knows the drift of his own arm –
Whether or not it lodges on her shoulder:
All her dear world's his habitat, and habit.

And this machine contracts them both, so perfect,
One stolen berry means a night of storms
And flight scattered next day in lumps and meltings
Of slashed upholstery, as if the sky

Had tried to move, and failed. Nothing moves freely
Here but the sea, old and unreconstructed.
It drowns the clover, mocks the poor, entices
Love's great protection racket to its housing.

INTRUDERS

Busy as paddles in liquid, ratchets in clocks,
   An army is making new clouds above the Falls,
   And the rain-thin quilt we wear for rest unravels
And some are secured, some trapped, behind rattled locks,

But none can wake. Adrift in the bickering flow,
   My thirst as riddled with questions as my sleep,
   I pick up the kettle, turn and almost leap
From the drawn blade flashed across the dawn-dark window.

SCHOOLGIRL'S STORY

The news stayed good until Monday morning
When a taxi driver was shot in the south of the city,
And his unnamed schoolgirl passenger injured.
Outside the window, clouds made changeable bruises
And spillings. Bad weather, taxi weather.
I picked up my dish, poured everything down the sink,
Unclogged it with bare fingers, ran for my coat,
Tried to flash back to how it used to be,
Hearing about these things every day of the week
And not feeling cold and sick and hot: the beauty
   Of being nobody's lover.

I could hardly stand up as I reached the school railings.
The clouds turned heavy again, opened fire
On my face and eyes with stinging grains to remind me:
Bad weather, taxi weather. *If it's not there*
I'll die, I'll scream, I'll run from here to Balmoral.
But the bike was neatly chained in the shed as usual.
The square-root of the frame, graceful, ice-blue,
Cut me the old two ways: her nearness, her distance.
The sky cleared. I began to look for her
Without seeming to. I stopped feeling sick for her.
   Another sickness took over.

THE LISBURN ROAD LIST
variations on a theme of Philip Larkin

Glooms of old stone between shops,
And flat oases that blaze
All night, as ubiquitous
As copywriters' full stops;
Churches and garages, both, in their different ways
Telling us this is a road going somewhere else:

And the buses to *Silverstream*
Via Shankill, crowded as far
As the bone-hard, low-church seats
Punishing each rear,
And the dozens of other competitive notions of 'home',
And the eyes gazing carefully down on each 'somewhere else':

And the dusks, as mournful and slow
As the queue at the road blocks,
A fire engine screaming through,
Past the heavily macintoshed barracks,
And the passers-by and the drivers thinking, What's new?
Thinking, Jesus Christ, why don't I live somewhere else?

And the gentler fantasies
For sale – a new colour scheme,
Facials, cheap holidays,
And, if all else fails, an ice-cream;
And the intricate, well-worked hills undeceived by the dream
That life could be utterly different, somewhere else.

And at last the ephemeral I,
Observant or bored, but never
Doubting that summer will soon
Arrive to unveil a vast sky
Of rooftops and trees and the hard bright light of that question:
Where is your love for the life you had somewhere else?

SNOWFIRE

The chimney stacks had been variously feathered
As the north wind pushed across Maryville Avenue,
Whitening a corner here, a full side there,
And sometimes leaving the odd stack disregarded.
The roofs were white, the clouds a little less so.
They moved on fast, as if from the scene of a crime
They'd merely witnessed, but would be accused of.
At first, I thought it was only chimney smoke
From a late-night hearth, trying to join the cloud-rush.
Then came a flashing, lit from beyond the apex.
Something on fire? It was bright enough, but silent:
A fire can't work without muttering, carelessly
Giving itself away. And now the wind
Was gushing up and up, and the roofs were dissolving,
And all the street was fainting and dazzling itself
In the dreamy blast. I watched till my face went under,
The fire wanted in, and I had to shut the door.

HEAD COLD

River-mouth world, is it really a surprise
That a new tenant has judged your sinuses
An ideal home? Your breath aches through his coal smoke
– Smell of the ancient tenderness of cities –
His fumey speeds sicken you like catarrh.

So many clouds, heroes of stone and shell –
The loveliest headache, if you could bear to look;
Every street laid with a different carpet,
Each garden its own mist of imagined spring,
Though a gloved thumb could wipe out any petal.

Strange city, doped and bright in your frosty vest,
Keep to your bed today, and fall in love
Again and again with the childhood illnesses
When your hands, unusually clean, turned the pages
Of adventures you could not possibly have.

ET INCARNATUS EST

Windows are often loneliest when lighted,
Their silvery plenitude a kind of treason.
They smile, they seem to offer invitation
Between the last-leafed branches, but their eyes
Are kind only if you possess the keys.
Journeys towards such stars are best diverted.

Desire, though, being the senseless thing it is,
I know a certain window from all angles
And frequencies. The city's whole *galère*
Contains no poorer version of stained glass,
But it's among the daily miracles
When I check anxiously, find it still there,
Glass being so promiscuous with its spangles,
And light so frail, in cities such as this.

I'm happiest when it's invisible,
Sunk in the fireless black of the night sky,
A lovely emblem folded, put away,
And nothing left more innocent and hopeful
Than life itself. *There's no epiphany,*
No magic room: this is an empty house.
I can unthrone it, if I trust that blackness.

But when, through the burnt-out December trees,
The window shivers dreamily, plays at being
An earth-bound moon, then shows me, bright and full,
That soft, shoulderly curve, that frame of grace,
I breathe like a runner though I'm standing still.
I know what it is to have been a king
Once, and now to be frightened of a stable.

Some windows pierce the flesh but this, when lighted,
Is flesh itself, those fluids, sighs, word-world.
Other lights vanish or become blurred.
This burns the mind – not light, but living eyes,
Faultless, candid, where my last hope dies,
A child of hell, its death never completed.

GENIUS LOCI

And through the blind glass that swings over every threshold
    I meet her eyes, touch her sleeve in an unfelt greeting,
And all the sad elms at their winter soliloquies strive
    To copy her gestures, the grace of her clarification.
Each passage of footsteps insists on my terrified waiting
    Because she is all these opacities and rehearsals.

And in all the bright precincts we claimed, the ingenuous windows
    That gazed at the sky and saw nothing are shocked into candour
Again as my hand cups a waterfall, studies a burning,
    Refining the one possibility, blatant, addicted,
And my lips brush a snow so unsettled and warm, with such lack
    Of demand, there is scarcely a trick of the air or the climate.

And if as I hurry home, rain-dazzled, down the long road
    With its blown-about pearls and its tapestry rucksack of hills,
She's there at the bus stop, shivering, cloud-breathing, earthed,
    Waving an uncertain hand to attract my attention,
It's not in a wish to avoid her that I almost pass her;
    Simply, reality's never itself but a vision.

I have held her and lost her and lost her so questionably
  There isn't a stone unbereft or unconsecrated.
All the hurrying cabs catch her up to some frangible safety:
  All the hedges weave gardens for her. She is every wind blowing,
Each darkness that's dressed in an impulse of light or water –
  An identity left, for a dying moment, wide open.

CLOUDING THE BORDERS
view from a train window, Belfast–Dublin, March 1992

The small hills glow their rain-deep green
In March as, in November, those
That hugged the sky round Iniskeen,
And fixed clay padlocks on our shoes.

Newry – where clouds already trust
Frail bodies to the most distant peaks.
North's westering gaze relaxes. Mist
And heather do their vanishing tricks.

No shadow of this landscape's mine:
No stick of it estranges me.
Kavanagh sowed his hills with coin.
We share the transient legacy.

I watch a ewe fold round her lamb,
Her brownish, and its snowy, fleece
Making in soft, unbroken form
The oldest word for *native place*.

CURRICULUM POETICA

Fountains are mostly light:
    A lough or tarn
Is the bland, incomparable
    Centrefold
Where breathless mountains yearn:
    Waterfalls dramatise
Earth's slightest *Oh*.
    But a stream, star-crossed,
Learns from the grass in its eyes
    Its profile's low.
Good enough to undazzle
    To the valley's level,
Still it's begrudged:
    Poor tinkling harper,
Pebble-prospector, tapster
    To witch and woad-man;
Hanger-out in the sticks,
    Grateful to be lodged
In cul-de-sacs blessed by
    Local voluminous slops.
How can it shine without sky,
    Without fire, foam over,
Lusty as loving-cups
    At the gods' table?

Mud is its pulse if mud
    Its course and kiddle,
Its art, a lament
    In curious hieroglyphs
Some clever-clogs will propose
    Is just the usual
Nattering on about
    Old roots, lost nymphs,
    And, anyway, in prose.

ANTRIM ROAD DREAM-HOUSE

The house hangs in the balance of our pockets,
As near, as far, as a remedy for cancer
Or love-in-absence, when we climb its core
To open rooms like gifts you rarely find
In January. A wing of summery light
Sheers up the highest wall, sinks to the raw
Wood of the staircase like a contract signed
In sky, a god's impulsive, longed-for answer.
Room, it says: room to repair homes broken
In haste, to be together and yet spacious,
Hospitable . . . The frame jolts forwards, then.
A wailing car warns us not to forget
What quality of mercy holds the keys
Of all this luxury, suspense, regret.

A SMALL INCENDIARY DEVICE ON EGLANTINE AVENUE

After the bang, seven globes flowered softly
On their seven stems, curving
Tall above the roofs and the long street.
Hot grain ran down the night in fading tracks
And a stick with which some child
Had touched the sky fluttered
Star-burned to our feet.

TWO WINDOWSCAPES
for Jean Bleakney

1

I watched a pulse of rainbow as it faded,
A sky-traced heartbeat, strong at first, but failing
And lost before my light-enchanted cones
Could mix the waves, my mind still lost for labels.
A rainbow's something else than seven plain tones.
It's less like paint than pastel, hazy, shy
With in-between shades, namelessly embraided.
That's why it seems so human and so tender.
A rainbow surely views us through the eye
Through which it's viewed – the cataracts, the floaters,
The weather and the weather-dazzled panes.

2

The sky was milk, plum-frozen to the bottle.
Suddenly, it had drained. The light went dead.
Something was slowly puzzling out the world,
Groping along strange airways, lost, and then
Boldly it took possession. Like a playground
My window teemed, all moving, all enchanted.

Original human sin – to be enchanted:
To see a freckled girl emerging where
The laurel glowered, North her safe white house,
Apollo soft and sullen in Ash Wednesday
Shrouds, knowing his place: to say there's hope
Or faith, at least, in the flurry of that sparrow
Who skims the yard wall, shivers so strongly up
Through the rich caves of the cotoneaster
It seems she's got a site marked out, already
Becoming fact among the water-nests
The snow keeps fixing and dissolving there.

SUMMER TIME BEGINS
for Joan Newmann

In a surprise of light
My chimney props its shadow
On the house-front opposite,
And the shadow-stack lets flow
An upward skitter
Of dirty curls, unstable
As local crosswinds.
If smoke and shadow-smoke
Changed place, how could we tell?
And which sign to trust:
The hills' milky sheaves
Of blizzard, swept low
By the gale's cutter?
Or the slow-widening
Harebell dusk that says
Kind days will soon come
Newly relaxing through
Each loaf-small home,
No smoke, no shadow-fire
Riddling, deriding,
But all we dared hope for
Made tangible: a second
Chance, an extra hour?

THE FIRST STORYTELLERS

They said there was a house, and something in it
Formed by the satin-finish light would give
An indoor courtyard, by the dusky sift
Of irons welcoming fire, and duckdown, sleep.
There was a rind as well, where pigeons shuffled
And shook their iris ruffs, and lived aslant,
Happy as slates, as clouds in a cloudy heap.
Some say that Time had found a place to live,
But Earth would not move in, so no one did,
Though there was flesh, and blood, and voice, and feeling,
As the first frightened witnesses declared,
A scalded hand, a shadow on the ceiling,
Senses that knew light died each day, and grieved
And invented a demon to be tender with.

TÍR FÁ TONN

   I was plunged in your dampest mood, my face had pearled over
Like the skin of an aeroplane suddenly scarfed by cloud.
   A second higher, I found your shining mirror.
Rose petals stained us, as if we had swallowed too quickly
   Too much new wine, and we were a compact, opened
Shyly as Venus's shell. Well, that day's skin is all dust now.
   We've rendered to Cloacina, who weaves the world,
The gifts that are hers, and the troubled streams of those fingers
   I stilled without touch have become the geologist's nightmare –
   A rock formation unique to vanished islands.

IRIS AND THE HAILSTONE

None of the weather-stirring hills predicted
She'd pick the stone up, turn it idly round.
She was dressed in maps, and yet she'd never read
Of rainbows being started in a hand.

Unnoticed, unforeseen, the stone thinned
To a bleb of dew, like Odras when she fell
As a little startled rain at Morrigan's yell.
This time, too, there was a cry to estrange
Matter from its laws: then a great arm
Of rainbow stemming from a seared palm,
A rainbow stemmed, a stone tossed out of range.

BEST CHINA SKY

A primrose crane, a slope of ochre stacks,
Stencilled on tissue-thin
Blue, and, flung between
Two worlds, a sword-flash rainbow,
The cloud it lies against
Metallic as its topmost skin,
And, round the eyes of hills,
The tender bluish-green
That quickly yellows.

The prism comes and goes:
Wonderful stain, transparency of art!
A smoke-wraith sails right through it.
But now it strengthens, glows and braves its span,
You'd think it was the rim
Of some resplendent turquoise plate,
Offering hills and cranes and streets and us
Fancies designed to melt
As our fingers touched them

PRAYER FOR NORTHERN IRELAND

Night, be starry-sensed for her,
Your bitter frost be fleece to her.
Comb the vale, slow mist, for her.
Lough, be a muscle, tensed for her.

And coals, the only fire in her,
And rain, the only news of her.
Small hills, keep sisters' eyes on her.
Be reticent, desire for her.

Go, stories, leave the breath in her,
The last word to be said by her,
And leave no heart for dead in her.
Steer this ship of dread from her.

No husband lift a hand to her,
No daughter shut the blind on her.
May sails be sewn, seeds grown, for her.
May every kiss be kind to her.

II

HOLDING PATTERN

STANZAS FOR A NEW START

Home for a long time fought with me for air,
And I pronounced it uninhabitable.
Then, in an old tradition of reversal,
I understood I'd left my future there.

I chased across the badlands of recession:
I'd make a bid for any cuckoo's nest
That sang the joys of owner-occupation.
No loan shark lacked the details of my quest.

Now it's acquired refinement. It's a passion
Long-pursued, a serious late career.
I've shelved my dreams of contract and completion.
Haste doesn't suit the eternal first-time buyer.

Home, after all, is not a simple thing.
Even indoors there should be garden voices,
Earth-breaking rootage, brilliant mirroring,
A constant foliation of loved faces.

Doors are a must, but let them make a palace,
Let each room smile another, on and on –
The glittering, the plain, the small, the spacious,
The sacred and the haunted and the one

Hope rests her case in – windswept, cornerless.

KILKENNY CASTLE

    Over the bridge it appeared –
a castle grown from the same mild stone,
    rounding a net of fine rain –
a castle that gazed, shivering, back from the river.
    I crept between those walls
of stone and stone-brown water
    where small swans paused and circled,
and climbed to the cup-shaped window
    of a high, lit room.
Ancestral portraits slanted looks at me,
    but I was not besieged.
I wore the castle as if it were mine,
    the breadth of its kingdom fallen
beneath my gold-dressed hands
    that were white like swans, and clean,
though the rain hung dark with twilight
    and the moss deepened on paths
between the listing black headstones
    down in St Canice's churchyard.

                      1976

RAGLAN WEIR

A simple man arrived in town . . .
'Adventures in the Bohemian Jungle', Patrick Kavanagh

1

We pass churches and town squares, we circle a crush of poppies
And a customs shed, and have reached my stony country.
Everything's as it was – the hump of the lane that twists
Suddenly away like a creature shying,
The stepping down from the bus to begin that journey
Of infinite dread and tedium, which love is,
And follow wherever the weather carries you
In its dirty glove like a stubborn, unsuitable flower
To mark the place where all is buried. Or spoken.

2

You've taken the kiss from my mouth up the lane and out of sight.
The river-grass is flowing like grey hair
In a gale, each spine exposed,
Debased. The waters are teasing something, apart
From themselves, chivvying it towards the weir –
A lucky leaf! It will zigzag slowly over

That long plunge and leave its name on the sea.
I'm waiting for you to come back down the lane
Hiding the proof of your girlhood, a rustling pharmacy bag:
I'm smiling at my own disappearing smile.

MY DARK WINDOWS

1

The voice said: *Come on in.*
Here are your naturalisation
Papers. You're one of the chosen
Few. Wilkommen. Bienvenue.
Welcome to the land of the frozen-
Out. And I went on in.

2

Wiping her hands in the Arrivals Hall ladies,
She sighs to me in the mirror: 'Grand to be home!'
In another mood I'd smile: 'It certainly is.'
In another, I'd joke: 'It's grand *not* to be home.'
But today my tongue has found a troublesome root
Which it's bound to touch and touch till the point of pain.
I simply shrug and refuse to demonstrate
How different 'home' is on her lips, and on mine.

3

The slow dawn of familiarities:
Walking the length of a street too sparsely peopled
For the victory cut of its buildings:

Even at dusk, the complexions
Of stone and glass perilously heightened:
Windows that shine as women groom young men
To be poets of death: my dark windows: my pen
In the same place under the bed where it rolled
Three weeks ago: nothing at all to keep me
From language – neither the sound nor the silence, *home*.

A HICCUP IN THE HISTORY OF BELFAST

In my new city street-plan, the big names
Try to slip through the pages incognito,
Blending with the crowd. I corner them
Heartlessly: 'I've seen you on the news,
Sobbing, with rain and soldiers in your hair,
By the burning take-aways and the black taxis!'
They look askance and beg to be let go.
I stand and gasp the legendary air.

I make things stranger making them familiar,
Taking the plunge past windows in steel vests
Where a boxed blowlamp and a sponge seem settled
For life on a cardigan's well-buttoned breasts.
I'm served with rough aplomb, and think I'm poorer
Only because I took the reddish-tan
Ulster Bank five for a Bank of England ten.

When I get lost, it's on some new estate,
Fences hugged to the end of every path.
A danger to cartography, I'm met
By a man with food and anger in his mouth.
'Looking for somebody?' He gives no hint
Of registering my accent and odd manner,

But clears the air, shaping the road I want,
Then saunters back to his gate and watches me –
The afternoon's bad news that proved to be
Merely a hiccup in its Sunday dinner.

NOVEMBER 1991

ST PETER'S WELCOMES THE PEACE WALKERS

Mini-skirted sixth-formers smile in the doorway,
Rattling donated boxes of Tunnock's Caramel Wafers.
Across the hall, their mothers and grandmothers
(The kind of women churchmen of all colours
Call 'our ministering angels') work with teapots.
The young priest welcomes the Methodists from the Shankill:
'We even painted the walls, look – just for you!'

I sit with two crisp-denimed Catholic women.
And soon we're friends, chatting about 'Queen's':
Maybe I've come across their student-children?
An older woman hovers, wants to join in
But won't sit down. She says she's not a marcher,
So it's not right: displays her ruined slippers.

'I'm on three types of pills,' she says, 'It's dreadful,
So it is. Abyssinia Street. A hell-hole.
D'you really like Belfast? Are you going to be staying?
I'm frightened to go out.'
                          'Couldn't you move',
One of the women says kindly, 'to the suburbs?'

Something collapses in the long silence.
Call it religion. Say what emerges, naked
And guileless as the orange walls, is Class.

OLD FRIEND, NEW ADDRESS

The self-despairer had frequently dreamed about
That easy stroll into the bombs and bullets.
He thought: *I'm in the right place, there's not a doubt.*
And shivered – *The wind, the rain, the mean little streets.
It must be the right place.* But his voice was faint
With the cowardice of hope as he called out:
*Which way do I go now? How do I pay my toll
At those unmanned checkpoints, at the wide wide gate?*

A SINGER TOO SOON
in memoriam J.S.

March has no summer manners.
The fragrance of grass at first cut
Is the gale's first hostage.

Unwillingly solo beside
The lough, the little bird
Has risked the gold of his life.

But the frost claws back the whole bet.
There will be no feast, no nest.
Or not today. And never for you, bright blackbird.

BOATING IN A BORDER COUNTY

Windless January dawn: the long rose-gold
Pulse across the lough so regular
It might have been an athlete's ECG.
The air glowed blue; even in the shed
Something filled the muddy pane like sky
Dreaming of itself.
                      You said: 'Too heavy!'
'Och, no,' the owner said. 'But she wants cleaned.
She's not been touched the year.' You both kept on,
But I kept on against the two of you,
Woman enough, for once, to get my way.

The oars slither fractiously as you struggle
To get a grip, and then they're under orders,
The boat tastes open water, and we're moving
Sweet as a late quartet's deep-carved legato.
Your gaze relaxes past me into pleasure.
This is your art, reflexive as the waves,
And like an art ingrained the shore goes with us,
Shuffling contours, altering a tree line,
Losing one white farm, adding another,
But never past redemption, as we steer
Horizonwards, our quest, of course, an island.

Those distant, sombre, unrequiting islands!
– Mythic as winter wheat till we get near
And watch them fall apart like old rush-mats,
Such sloppy nests as wouldn't house a duck egg.
But when at last one offers foothold, homesick
Almost at once, we roam in circles, back
Through the thin coppice to our sidling craft
Whose dizzy wobble we construe as welcome,
And there we broach picnic like two babies,
Dandled, replete with liquidness and light.

We barely noticed, but a trail of mesh,
A few splintery stakes, have placed us south
Of where we woke, doubled our emigration.
I want to smile, imagining contraband
So simply shipped, but when I glance across
To see your happiness, that other border,
As vague, as definite, shivers between us:
The soul stain of your cancer diagnosis.

A turn so sharply wrong ruined our maps,
Roughed up our boat at first and nearly sank us.
Today, it marries us. The shudder passes,
And it's as if you've rowed us out to where
The future meets us, settling round our breath.
Enough, it sighs, enough!
                      Our precious future . . .
It was a form of childhood; we could leave it
On such a day, in such circumference.

FERMANAGH, 1995

WINTER TRAVEL

On the dirtiest winter nights they keep arriving;
Bringing the smell of snow, they squeeze themselves in
At the too-few miniature tables, flushed with achievement,
Or queue for carry-outs, collars ear-high and dripping,
Shuffling a slushy thaw right back to the painted curbstones.
The cars swap spaces, the counter girls swerve and signal
Faster, have to lean farther, have to dig deeper
To fill the gleaming flavourscoops, build up the pokes and cartons
With doubles and triples of carefully picked, fairly sick, combinations:
And in tucked-away terraces all over town, where the sleet
Is flowing in heavier folds and not even a robin
Would dare his faint rose ember, his watery winter flute,
A van, tall as an ambulance, nearly as pale,
But in no hurry at all, is panting around
The corners, lighting the blizzard, the shadows, stopping
By windows where Advent is fairy-lit advert, to peal
A humdinger peal of a glockenspiel reel that unwraps
The children from the TV sets, hurries the grownups, shivering,
Grumbling, searching their purses, beginning to die
All the same for the tooth-shocking, tongue-tricking, slippily swift,
Yet measured, dissolve. Yes, pleasure is snatched like a windfall
These nights when the city goes dancing in the ball-room of ice-cream.

ABSENT WEATHERWOMEN

I'd like to believe your hills controlled the weather.
I don't disbelieve. I know the clouds
That bloom and fade faster than weekend bruises
Are not marshalled by the weathermen
Nor the military, for all their satellites
And calculation. Those that squeeze their eyes
Tearful with prayer don't cause the mists to thicken.
I know the harebell dawn is not God smiling
Encouragement to his momentary chosen,
And that it isn't women that cause the rain
To daub and chill this city in its heartbreak
Maytime – nor the absence of those women.

THE ISLAND

Its contour rises softly as the death wish
When the Gartan mother sings her lullaby.
Belatedly you learn all seas confess

This landfall, though some blame it on the sky.
The harbour's rumoured safe as flax. But first
Some fate or fury, not to be confused

With Scylla and Charybdis, lesser Greeks,
Must check your passport and may hurl you starboard
To the gut-strewn kippering sheds of Nemesis.

That's why I pace the shore, procrastinating
With needles, mermen, dockside politics,
So Englishly. I do like being beside

The seaside but the sea's another thing.
One mouth could sing my uncertain own to it
Multas per gentes, kiss goodbye to bookish
Skills like divination and safe sex.

FROM A LEXICON OF UNLIKELY COUPLES

Looking up *dene*, I saw it stretch a slender
    Palm across the downscape, north, to *dun*:
Southron and Scotsman, borrower and lender,
    Lay cheek to cheek as two sides of a coin.
Next, stranger still, *desire* and *lack* made one
    Honeymoon pair, a Paolo and Francesca,
Whirled among fiery stars, yet never warm,
    Their special hell the absence of all friction,
    Their married name *desideratum*.

NOTE
Southron was the term used by Basil Bunting to refer to a person from the South of England.

TO POETRY

My darkest eye, the one I've never seen
In any glass, changes the day with you,
Colouring bridally, though out of season,
Like hills in sudden scarves of frost or bracken.
It knows your fiercest winter hex, but stays
Patient, snow-lidded, meeting dark with dark.
It loves the rose-bright pulse of you in health:
Its vein runs to your heart, picks up the song.
It sees you best when everyday eyes sleep,
But should these daily eyes lose sight of you
The meanest light will never meet my road.

HOUSEWARMING

I will not light a fire until you come.
   It'd be too absurd to hear the flames
   Trickling their tongues over your bodiless names:
The hearth won't be disturbed, unless you come.

I will not cook a meal until you come.
   Love cooks. Solitude warms up frozen things.
   The gas, with a cheerful *whoosh*, jumps into the rings
– The only miracle, unless you come.

I'll dust, I'll get the place immaculate,
   Then watch the trains, listen for taxis. Clouds
   And sun will stroke my house, dusk bring it shades,
But these are not its soul. I'll watch and wait.

And when you've come, and gone, when small flames sigh
   And kiss the broken mirrors of the coal,
   Pulling the warm bricks round it like a shawl,
   The house will say: it's a strange thing, a soul:
A kind of hollow shining, a choked cry.

TO BREAK HOUSE RULES

And what if these empty rooms had been love's house?
What if there'd been a second soul in them
Instead of the old stones and bones of verse –
A daughter-soul, with its own quick-slipping bloodstream?
And what if she had been mistress of this house,
Shaking its basalt spars in a snowstorm of moments,
Spinning that garden of frozen energy
So that it sprang and branched and a palace blossomed?
Who's to say a palace was never love's tomb?
Who's to say a tomb was never love's palace?

PROMETHEAN

When even in my dreams you turned your back
And flung the gift that I alone could tease
Out of your eyes, to any fool but me,
I knew for certain I was dead – or good as.
Now I could see the vulture fashioned by
The greediest drinkers, now he filled the day
More than a fridge of bottles, now his talons
Seized and strode the white harp of my ribs,
And with his plunging beak he stripped and stripped
Every last song from my imagination.

STRANGE WOUNDS

No more screeched vespers, no more hell-holes through cloud,
   Only – for the unsleeping – troubles of thought.
Burned-in memories, for most; for luckier others, blurred
   Or second-hand. I am the luckier sort,
Shamed by the mind which paces and almost breaks
   On an image not of war but of two pillowed heads
   Parted by half a mile, and a cliff of words.
     And I think: what life would be, if wishes could bring
     Audible tender whispers from wretched beds!
I would be human again, like a city no longer mad,
   Though its spirit aches,
  And the longed-for quietness not so hollow a thing
If, from the heart of lost friendship, we promised to add
Our stitch towards closing this strange new wound called peace.

THE BURIAL
in a forest of County Antrim

Once fairy-struck in pine-dim light I watched
A fern become alive, tremble and speak
A thousand contradictions, terrified
Of how I stared until I prayed it back
To some tired metaphor that it could bear –
The quaint *fiddlehead*, the ancient *pteron*.

WHERE THE RAINBOW ENDS

Halfway down Cranmore Park, it becomes clear
    That the road is heading straight for the roots of the hills:
The trees descend like a wavy slide at a fair:
    The city's abandoned, green will flourish for miles.

Up go the hills to heaven, as sinlessly
    As pets, with their velvet flanks, their stripes and tufts,
And down, down slips the road, black gravity
    Tarring my feet while my gaze, free-floating, lifts.

The trees soon tire of the game. They block the way
    Scots pines, chestnuts, larches – glorious things
But proud and a little cold, inclined to weigh
    And sift their shade above fussy gardenings.

And then there are so many chimneys saluting the sky
    Their fists have all but obliterated the blue
Not to speak of the green, which looked so near, so true,
    But now seems merely the memory of a trompe l'oeil.

Mourn as I might, I haven't any choice
    But to turn my rise to my fall, and let the hills
Dissolve, as a face dissolves into a house,
    Leaving the stranger nothing but roads and rules.

A LABEL

*written after reading Brendan Kennelly's address
to the 'Cultures of Ireland' conference*

Here, where people tell me I'm a Brit
(Meaning 'You're one of us' or 'You're a shit')
I think back to my convent-schoolgirl art
Of being partisan and yet apart.

Protestant, but with nothing to protest
About – except the ban on going to Mass,
I was the Catholic wannabe of our class,
Spot-on in every catechism test.

Filling in forms for work when I arrived
In Belfast, seeing 'Name of primary school',
I nudged myself away: not you, you fool:
Outsiders aren't *religiously perceived.*

'She gets enough God at St Winefride's,'
My mother, sheepish, told the minister
Of the local church we stepped in once a year.
He smiled: 'I'm sure God isn't taking sides.'

I'm the 'Don't know' who puts down 'Humanist'
In God-shaped boxes now. My deep debate

Is not whether gods or goddesses exist.
I try to be the mother of my fate

And not its whinging kid: I think I'm tall
Enough to count as self-responsible.
And yet – and here's the silly paradox –
I sometimes think I'd like a labelled box.

So Brendan, though I realise your address
Was aimed at more God-fearing types than me,
Those words you coined spoke to my oddity,
They took me in, made 'exile' matter less:

And next time it's a God-shaped tag I want,
I'll try your *Protholic* – no, your *Cathestant*.

SPARK CITY

I'm joined to the city by wires I can't disconnect,
Hooked to its ghostly looms and pulleys, imbroiled
In CableTel's snaking ambitions, swung to the oxters
Of shipyard cranes and dropped again to the Lagan's
Sky-sleeked hinges: I ring with the sweaty switchboards
Receiving code words and weather forecasts and when
The massed amps woke amazed in that waterfront shrine,
Proud as a new bride's first unsunken soufflé,
I was wired to the larynx of Kiri Te Kanawa.
This is an air I can use, however darkly it's laced
With the gush of burnings in which you detect the harsh
Flesh-smell of hope as it perishes once again
And at the same time hotly refuses to perish.
I've heard of a city where everyone speaks to each other
And my head buys the crack and the crackle, high as a telegraph pole;
My body grows taut like the rope twined round the sleek stalk
By a small girl spinning herself off the Ormeau Road,
Off the planet, in fact, in a street near the shop that sells
An Phoblacht, the street that keeps my tongue in my mouth,
Short as its Irish name, long as its memory.

The city's my floating root, my family of no one
– No Christmas cousins, no fondling parents for tea-stained
Kitchen Sundays, no grandchild to tug me to playschool,
No ancestor un-decayed, no tribe betrayed.
In every street it's awarded me, pinning another
Name on my pincushion heart – Sans Souci, Moonstone,
Maryville, South Parade, Great Northern, Greenore,
Next, who knows, I had no name but stranger,
The woman alone, but not like the others, the grey-heads
Whose children were raised here, all the various young,
Their families at bay but watchful, biding their time like the hills.

I was like them in another life, but there
I was less than I am – or who I am most had nowhere
To kick off its shoes and spread itself and sigh *home*.
This is the city I gave my most difficult self.
And, coming back, it's always a self re-made
Gradually from the small fields, the cameras and sheep and blue
Composures of lough and mountain, the rock 'n' roll
Of voices that crest in a triumph that puzzles the down stroke:
All motley and rusting elderly parts reassembled
And rainbow-greased, I'm charged by the first wild sparks
Upwind in the gold-rush canyon of Great Victoria Street:
So to the parks, my lovely crossing-places,
And the ochre bricks and the ball games in dusty entries
Where at last I find what's mine, the fathomless secret ignitions.

Then dusk and I will listen, and hear the summer
Practise its tight-faced squealing, its stamp and thunder.
Outrage and beacons will blaze, but I'll look at the sky

At least till a brick comes dancing through my window,
And write out my IOUs in a primitive, garrulous metre,
And beg that nobody yet pulls out the wires,
Demanding what right I have as a citizen
To claim the place where imagination fires.

NO MAN'S LAND

Places are perfect for belonging to:
They can't get up, they can't walk out on you.
Whatever clever tricks the planners do,
The same old place, the pained old face, smiles through.

You can walk out on places, certain they
Won't mind or try to find you. Places stay
Put; however far you move away,
One of those streets will take you back one day.

And if it's been unmapped or wrapped in steel,
With tripwires lurking for the mortal heel,
Run down or stunned with an official seal —
Pick up your place and walk. Its weight is real.

A place is home, however dim or dead.
It's much less trouble than a double bed.
You think your place is someone's heart or head?
Forget it. Love geography instead.

CHARACTERS
reading Elizabeth Bowen in Cork City

So often, as day ends,
It's not to lamp-warmed faces we return,
Not to our hungry friends,
But to the children of imagination.
They live in us like memories,
And yet belong to nowhere we could name
In our own stories.
They can't converse
Except by weaving patterns like their sun
– A strange, interior sun
Across their strange, dark-edged, interior days –
Yet we know their voices.
Lock both doors, now, curtain the river. Night
In real-time, with its tracer fire
Of meetings and desire,
They've learned, like us, to hate.
Permit them this, their only happiness
Of knowing they became our only light.

WHITE-WATCHING IN CORK CITY
for Sinn Féin

Sea gulls that sipped
The outflow, searched the tip,
Lift shining caps and sleeves
For the sun's approval.
Even on Ring Mahon strand,
You could fill sieves
With clean shell-petals.
Is nature a witch?
Abused and weary, still
Her whites excel,
Shine without bleach.
But what of these
Fine human feathers –
The satin alphas,
The snowy-braided
Manes, the lamp post doves
That daintily fly down
Onto sticks paraded
By our local dreamers,
Wearing their spring fleece:
How white is their peace?

MARCH 1996

CONVERSATION WITH A SEA GULL
in memoriam Joseph Brodsky

Poem-maker, your guild disbanded, not one
    Man left at his station:
Love-adept, at last unbefriended, no-win
    Your situation,
So what if some cloud from your most Aquarian mood,
    Or a snowflake of brain,
Drift above Shandon, prospecting for Leningrad
    Through thickening rain,
Puzzling in vain for the wobbly Venetian *O*s
    Of arch-backed embraces,
The aristocratic self-disregard of *palazzo*s?
    Such weathers aren't voices.
Say the feathery soul of your river-love just gave a cry
    As it dived from the railing –
A gull is a Soviet type, mass-produced, sly.
    Your wings would be flailing.
Whether nature plays God is still what I want to know.
    Can selves be re-formed
Like the river from rain? And now I can hear it – abseiling
    In spirals down from your vast oratorical

Rucksack – the question. *The question, Kerol,* you're saying,
  Is surely rhetorical?
The self is – well – imaginary, and it will go
  Nowhere – or wherever imaginings go.

CORK, 1996

SISTER LOVE

Let me go south with you into forgiveness.
In the dark of the coach I'll mend our broken hearts
With a perfect pin from my handbag's Tír na nÓg.
We'll prop the bar though the farmers throw us long looks,
Your eyes burdened, opaque as a city river.
And then, with barely a shrug, you'll stalk off alone
And dip and rise and become as lost in hills
As any grocer's daughter, dressed for the Lords,
Her Penney's skirt kissing her clayey heels.

A DAY IN THE LIFE OF FARMER DREAM

In the morning light I stand outside my limits,
With equanimity survey the fields,
The thorn-hemmed acres that I call my land.
Some are ploughed, some newly sown, some thick
Already with astonishing wheat: some wait
Under a tat of kelp, or bask in clover.
In the morning light I lightly weigh my tasks:
A strong-jawed tractor stands on the hilltop,
The day burns to be off, time is enormous.
What happens in between I couldn't say,
But the grass has grown, and I return on foot,
A tinker or a tourist, one who gambled
Perhaps, or dawdled over skip and scrapyard,
Or slept because the blue was cradle-curved,
And ownership a gleam under a shawl.
Back west, the lying day projects its harvest
Of goldshine; dew is deepening round each stone,
And mist and I will climb the hill, soon, seeking
A house that wears the plume of our dissolving.

AUTUMN HAIKU

1

Already, they blush,
The nervous eye-witnesses
That have seen too much.

2

Through thin yellow skin
Their green souls shine. Oh burning
Envy, hardest fall!

3

They dress for the dance.
Tenaciously, with torn fans,
Finger-hooks dally.

4

If these fires were fast,
And held the deep glow of peat;
Ice, ever tearful,

5

And hope, seasonless,
We'd declare it paradise
And no loss – at first.

6

Float your black net, catch
The last great lavender sky,
Watch your children die.

THIRST FOR GREEN

The trees are coming into leaf
Like something almost being said . . .

'The Trees', Philip Larkin

Now their dreams are letting them through to the top of their wet black sleep
Though nothing has heard them stir yet. Only the hyacinths beading
The bed-fringe of each gaunt Kali, patient to match
Five o'clock's lavender cloud, and, along the square,
The lights coming on in the seminar rooms a little later each week
Seem to remember the trees will soon be awake.

It's easy to measure, still, the uneasy length of that street,
From the windows arched like prayers round the heavily pencilled
Shamrock and tudor rose, to the wish that, whatever occurred
In my chest, it was less like the trapdoor drop when the noose
Drags up a life in its fullness for the last breaking,
And hemp says to bone: your incident is closed.

If it had just been a season, a hibernation,
This grief-time, why is it growing, why is it rhyming with leaf-time?
There should be haulage and transport, the great distribution of sap
Flowing like silk through the restless loom of veins:
The story was written in water, I'd say, but listen, it rebegins
With a sigh from the root to the crown's wind-shaken, smoky tip.

But something as tight as despair winds round the throats of these thoughts.
Pathogens crowd where a thirst is disturbed by rain.
Is something wrong with the rain? It pales, refusing to climb
Towards the clamped buds in their dream of making light.
And then I remember: elms are cursed, spoor-thick with an old disease.
And the spring crawls in like nothing on earth, with no leaf-heraldries.

AN ANSWER

How perilous is it to choose
Not to love the life we're shown?

'Badgers', Seamus Heaney

Perilous as two planes on one flight path,
As the cry of a mother for her mother, lost,
As faith in a man who's sleeping with his past,
As the Bay of Biscay in an inflatable life raft.
When, like a soldier, you ran from one collapsed
Study-house to the next, you sinned against
The protocol of an ambitious host,
But not, I think, against the Holy Ghost.

WORDS

Once, conversation seemed so kind a thing,
It was not less than the leafing heart of May;
It was not more than age could ask of spring:
This fresh-formed light of a last-year self's decay.

But half the words were fingering edgy stones
And sticks, thick with the wit for opening bones.
Into the heart of the plot I could not fence
They dug the pure and violent poison: silence.

A FEAST OF EPIPHANY

The god of human love was king of kings
Then, to our wooden classroom, and wherever
Our finger moved, a small star cruised with us,
Nervously eyeing shapes beyond the wind.
I must shed epochs if I'd see it now,
Or feel the weight of gifts which filled my hands
– Which, as we'd learned, brought nothing. Is there mercy
In any universe for us who knelt
Crownless among the hungry, kicking lambs,
And touched the star, we numerous underlings
Who believe, now, in all kinds of imaginary things?

SYBIL YAWNS

I got there through a time slip and although
The mortals stared in horror at my madness
(Everyone hates untimely youth) I stuck it.
The years crawled over me, disguised as years.
Then I saw people had the same delusion:
Time didn't move for them, but kept its usual
Once upon, decent as murder stories
Filed by old hands to kill old time, young nonsense
About some war they lost their bloody heads in.

TWO BELFAST BEASTS

1 Paranoia

Yes, all roads lead to an Ulster Bank or a hill,
But the only way there's through Paranoiaville.

Now Paranoia's a wild colonial beast:
He rules in the West, he's got dens all over the East,

And he's so at home in the North, it's sometimes said
He grows another equally paranoid head.

In the South he's lying low, but he's seen at parties,
Boozing with poets and other mad arty-farties.

So visit that city of riches if you will,
But remember you're entering Free Paranoiaville.

2 The Ice Dragon of Great Northern Street

Some things simply can't be got right.
For all that I tried to research
The ways of my solid-fuel heater,
The fuel never wanted to catch.

My lighters, my high-grade coal
And my coal-coaxing implements
Might have been buckets of soil
And a draft of discouragements.

It's not that it never took pity:
Sometimes, the great northern pipes
Would murmur a small northern ditty
Hushing my huge southern gripes.

But I couldn't rely on it ever;
The same kind of treatment next day
Would leave us both cold. So I never
Learned when I should turn away

And when to keep stroking my dragon.
I suspected some faulty design
(Either the dragon's, or mine).
Though I'm just the usual woman,

And it seemed just the usual fire,
We couldn't reach mutual delight.
With the staunchest resolve and desire,
Some things simply can't be got right.

THE PHOTOPHOBE

A house can be haunted by those who were never there
If there was where they were missed.

'Selva Oscuras', Louis MacNeice

You have to leave a haunted house. Of course.
And so she did. She found one with no ghost,
No perfumes, chills, nobody to be missed,
And nothing to be kept but regular hours.

Plain views look in, confirm their lack of past:
A toytown bridge, one figure glancing over;
Electricity's tall exoskeleton;
A pine's display of brushes, the red downpour
Of dogwood, and four windows like her own –
A random hand she's no wish to uncover.

She wants a word-tight solitude, not response.
Her words have eyes, her views, blinds that displace
Each winter-morning dazzle of pin-point suns –
Her wasted breath, staring her in the face.

GHOST STORY

It happened to me once. Footsteps swirled through the dream,
Grew louder, stopped at my door, became the silence
I woke to. Heartbeats shook me. I remembered the one guest
You must never welcome, stepped from a raft of time
Carelessly drifting loose in the night-spaces,
The most powerful of all spirits, and not benign,
Though you'll long to open the door to her and greet her
As if she'd come home to you, your own dead happiness.

STREET SNAPSHOTS IN A NEW PEACETIME

Late afternoon is best, when the sun has softly sidestepped
To the other tradition, the one that sips black water,
Its head against the hills, half waiting, half asleep.

By now, the sky's so tired of appearing patriotic,
It yawns a teatime colour where the evangelist falls
Into his own happy grave, and the junkman rises again,
His one loud yelp expecting nothing more
Addictive than a day no longer treasured.

My childhood ragman wove among Routemaster buses,
Steamrollers, grown-up trikes, and other post-war traffic,
His pram wheels picking up shreds from the hay pancakes.
I never believed there was sense on my ragman's tongue.
When the words dawned I lost some god of language.

Junk, yelps the old man, Jesus, yelps the evangelist,
But across the street a different language is growing
In a blue-jerseyed, gate-swinging child who'll speak it tomorrow.
Surpassing herself, she'll remember all the details:
The stiff little horse on his flapping flag, the three bright antique curb-colours

LONG SHOT

The city that tried to be hope's capital drowses
In a bluish scum, perhaps being bathed, or printed.
As three new skeins trickle white from the cloudmakers' chimneys
And the first buses edge towards filmy heartland,
You would need more words than spires to be persuaded
That the usual business had tested its connections,
And finds them this morning in perfect working order.

TEA ON THE FIFTH OF JULY

In the countdown days, she agreed with several women
The merits of oestrogen over testosterone,
Then that seemed too black-or-white, too us-against-them,
So regretfully she abandoned the oestrogen
In favour of long baths, spliffs and chocolate (hot) –
Such stuff as would fell the feistiest patriot.
Under the influence, no doubt, she began to fashion
A joint so huge it was still a long way from ashen
By the time it had travelled the tremulous, sweet lip-line
From a terrace in BT6 to another in Portadown
And back. Old men were leaning against the murals
And vaguely planning cross-community fleadhs and festivals,
While the young saw reason at once and unravelled the charms
Of the two traditions known as 'one another's arms';
And if something somewhere was marching, it was only a poem
That was late for its tea, and anxious to get home.

THE SONG OF JACK FLAG

We blare them at meetings, we smear them on walls,
We pummel them into the littlest skulls
Who pedal them round on their tricycles –
    Our principles.

We pipe them, we drum them, we munch them in baps,
We put them on backwards like baseball caps:
We'll be strung up where the weather flaps
    For our principles.

And we'll dance like Jack Flag when he scissors the air
Screaming, 'Dead men do what the live don't dare!
We screw our own arses splinter-bare
    Like our principles!'

WORDS FOR POLITICIANS

The Party of Frogs is the Party of Toads
The Party of Corners, the Party of Roads
The Party of Gloves is the Party of Glands
The Party of Whispers, the Party of Bands
The Party of God is the Party of Good
If you haven't learnt that yet, you bloody well should

'Cos the Baseball-Bat Party's the Party for Learning
The Book Party's party to Naughty-Book Burning
The Bring-Back-the-Past Party's fighting for Progress
The Yes-No Brigade utters nothing but No-Yes
The Green Party's Pink and the Can Party Couldn't
And if you believe me you bloody well shouldn't

'Cos Doubt is the Party of Bold Self-Assertion
The Party of Faith is the Party-Sized Version
The Idiots' Party's the Party for Smarties
The Party from Hell is the Party of Parties
The Party for Fish is the Party for Bait
And you'd swallow anything, wouldn't you, mate

'Cos the Anything Party's the Party of Sellers
The Bendy Spoon Party's that Party of Geller's

The Party of Saddam's the Party of Freedom
The Party of Women is out – we don't need 'em
The Party of Lagan's the Party of Boyne
And if you don't like it you still have to join

'Cos the Party of Like-It's the Party of Lump-It
The Party of Muffin's the Party of Crumpet
The Bakery Party's the Party of Ormeau
The Sunny Twelfth Party's the Party of Lawn-Mow
The Party of Nine is the Party of Six
If not then there's nothing a penknife can't fix

'Cos the Party of Cut is the Party of Run
The Popular Front is a Party of One
The Smoke-Alarm Party's the Party of Fags
The Party of Gays is the Party that Drags
The PUP is a Party no doggie wants in
If you start a New Party don't think it will win

'Cos the Fresh Approach Party's the Party of Same
The Alzheimer's Party's forgotten its name
The Residents' Party arrives by the coachload
The Pesticide Party is really a Roachload
The Party of Bread's on the Party of Shelves
If you want some more Parties, twist words for yourselves.

TO HIS COY MISTRESS, FROM BEYOND THE GRAVE

*Cargoes, The Copper Kettle, Ruby Tuesday's,
Maud's, The Cello, The Manhattan Diner* –
These were the places (not
Very private, but none finer)
Where, in the 2020s, we would meet
For morning coffee or a teatime snack.
By then, we both wore black:
I'd learned to be discreet,
You, to be kind. And if the gossips still
Said I stared rather strongly in your eyes,
What was a stare?
At least it proved we were there.

It would have been eleven years, one week,
Past the millennium,
Before I'd touched your wrist –
Only to ask the time.
Another decade on, my withered cheek
Brushed yours to simulate
At the conclusion of each date
The Regulation Feminine Irish Kiss.
So we weren't enemies, it seemed, despite

The odd arthritic sulk, dyspeptic rage:
No debts, but those of age.

That famous winter struck in '29:
And took away our breath.
From *Bluebells* to the *Nonstick Frying Pan*
Our olde-worlde tips and mostly charming ways
Were mourned, but not for long. And when
In a plush-lined booth beneath
A mound where excavators had been poking,
Your walking stick and mine were glimpsed
Stiltedly necking,
So many centuries had elapsed
That who could blame us?
There was not one biographer to name us!

FRESH GARBAGE

That 'fresh' is Belfast irony, I suppose.
You could search from Kennington to Camden Town,
And not unearth a cave so backward-dreaming
Unless you somehow timewalked into those
Summers from '68 to '73
When the pirate stations promised you the news
Every hour, on the hour, and when news
Gave names to what you hoped the world could be:
Paris, Prague, San Francisco, Free Derry.

STITCHES IN TIME
for the women who worked on the Ards Community Textiles Project, 1995

Our world is stitched into time
And time has the needle hand,
With barely an inch of room
To put all our moments in.
The work was already begun
When a woman, a few days late,
Wondered, started to wait.

Our sex was cross-stitched in cells.
We doubled, diversified
Into lips and fingernails.
We hung ourselves upside-down,
Content to be anyone,
And drowsed on our silky tide
Till storm-waves ripped it undone

And we smashed the crystal of light
Headfirst. We had lots of voice.
We were bathed and buttoned up tight,
Buttoned from left to right.
We learned about Me and You.
We embroidered the facts. We grew
Taller, space became less.

When does the world get small?
There is no night to the day
At first, no limit to *girl*:
Then the tape-measured months dismay.
Hemlines go up to our thighs,
Mothers are tidied away.
Girls are cut down to size.

We are stitched into life. We flow
For love: then distant seas
Call love abroad. We must sew
Or weave our own long days.
Whether or not we wait
For Ulysses (always late),
Our task is Penelope's.

And it is ourselves we make.
Are the stitches strong? Will she break
Or tear? Will she keep us warm
Like a glove? Our lives are not nine
But living moments are born
From our hands when thread and rhyme
Stitch us in time.

THE LIGHTEST DANCER
to Michael Longley, on the publication of The Ghost Orchid

A bee, drawn earthwards
By the breath from a tuft of clover,
Went from choice to choice,
Fanciful, hovering.
There seemed no itinerary,
An improvisation, merely.
But, by the time it was over,
No flower had been left untouched,
And no flower, touched twice.

SONG OF THE GSOHS

We're the gsohs of Little Ads.
We're slimmish lasses, solvent lads,
And wltm other kind gsohs,
With a view to taking off our clothes.
Ala's our promise, though we're Ps,
NSs, Christians, or RCs.
Our gods have words like *sin* and *blame*,
But we're the grins skimmed from their shame.
Come giggle with us, nose to nose,
And found the future race of gsohs.

INSIGHT IN LAVERY'S

A harmless drug, a harmless friend?
– Never, till Homo's sappy end:
But if you need some harm, you mug,
Choose a young friend or an old drug.

DILEMMA

In the dusk of a northern summer, its soft impeachable white
False as the living-room satin inside a shell,
I begin to sway like the tongue of some horrible human bell
That must muffle itself and die, or shatter the night.

RIDDLE

Like cancer cells, ivy, arthritis,
Lips on a window, a lie,
A waistline, a stain you keep rubbing,
The spaces hands make to deny:
Like fire, and the rumour of fire,
Its nature is always to spread.
It will blossom in public and private,
And loves to take root in your head.

Answer: censorship

CÉILÍ IN BELFAST 9

Your man plays cool, your man plays safe
But wouldn't you like an acrobat, a tightrope-walking waif?

Your man mustn't know, but don't you ever go
For the disreputable charmer or the milk-white dairy-farmer?

Your man will never go, but couldn't you, even so,
Fall for a wheeler-dealer or a two-hand reeler?

You're fine, you're Belfast 9, but why shouldn't you
Go west, go south, go sip at the mouth of the wild child-stealer?

SANS SOUCI FLATS

I am my neighbours' lives, their woodwork parties,
The war dance of their lust, their shoe grenades,
The no-surrender dialogue of their doors.

My skull's the hollow kitchen where their Hotpoint
Scrambles the wash all night, and gender governs
Each quarrel in remorseless stereotype.

And what am I to them? An ancient deafness
Under the floor? A quaint old beam, or buttress,
Oak, of course, proof to all blasts and shaking?

I couldn't hope to speak their rip-tongued jabber,
Yet listening to them now's my one obsession.
In this, I'm an example to my country.

CHRISNIN GIFTS

Me Sarfa-the-River whine's got some Belfast vowels
By now, but it aint dead yet, not while we can cross
The wotjamacallit, *sheugh*, and Ole Muvver Lee still pulls
A pint of Watney's Brown in the Duke of York's.

That blank on the *A to Z*, down the Plumstead Road
– That's Woolwich Arsenal – stuck behind ten-foot walls
With a great big black steel gate, and two squat black steel shells
Sunk in concrete, one on guard each side.

They trooped through here for their 'call-up', aunts and cousins,
Dressed to the nines and getting the giggles. See,
It's offices now, top-secret, MoD.
– No chance for us to go snooping. Lousy work, munitions.

But at Charlton Pier where the Russky sub was packing
To head downstream for Folkstone, who should I meet
But an old great aunt of mine – well, the dead spit,
Skinny and permed and dyed and yakkety-yakking.

'Me son's a marine, we both worked on the sub,
Showing the tourists round, like ... an now I'm out of a job.
Ee's going off to is ship.' It was like in '46,
Not a barrel of fun for the girls sent back to the sticks.

Them blown-up empty sweetie-bags of war
Musta been what the fag-puffin Fates set down
Beside the engraved serviette ring, the silver brushes and mirror,
When I basked in me hyphened name and me chrisnin gown

To be tickled pink by 'the tale of the old iron pot'.
There was singsongs in shelters, Messerschmitts in the park.
'The war was murder,' they said, so you knew that what
They really meant was, 'Lor, but it was a lark.'

Well, I've tidied my tongue, flown back to my second home
And I'm peeking into gigantic paper-bags
Full of stale hot air and bull's-eyes and prophets of doom
And lads on the march, and an empire's worth of old flags.

ROUND TRIP

This must be home when a voice returns from floating
    And sinks into the dialect of a bay.
Its wonderment instantly becomes dismay.
    This must be home when a voice returns from floating
Out among islands, sheds protective coating,
    Achieves itself, then catches itself self-quoting:
'This must be home when a voice returns from floating
    And sinks into the dialect of a bay.'

INEDUCABLE

Looking out on that drenched street my heart
half-listening as I say not this again
it echoes *this again* and I continue
to look half-seeing am I not alive
to all rain does to stone isn't my passion
for being free for being sensible
to all rain does to stone isn't my passion
to look half-seeing am I not alive
it echoes *this again* and I continue
half-listening as I say not this again
looking out on that drenched street my heart

HOLDING PATTERN
(Belfast–London)

There were the rag-rug streets looking like silk
As light burst from a different angle, floating
The tiny mop-head trees on rafts of shade;
Old Thamsey, too, on form, busily twisting
Out of her rat-gnawn, matt-brown Gravesend stocking
To shake a rippling knee-bag for a brighter
Putney mood. That sudden rash of glitter
– Of sweat and spills and goosebumps – got me thinking
How, if you'd choose an island for its windows,
You'd go for this one, never mind the quick
Clearance of Aldergrove, the fields you reckoned
As space, the opened rainbow-mines you sank through.
And then I knew – this was my holding pattern:
To circle hopefully, never admitting
Before this moment (and not really now)
Which self, which well-embroidered plot, which mainland,
Which graveyard, I was travelling with my back to.